MW01711482

[redacted]

BRACEBRIDGE PUBLIC LIBRARY

J 641 .357 Ill

Illsley, Linda.
Herbs and spices / Linda Illsley ; illustrations by John Yates. -- Hove, England : Wayland, 1990.
32 p. : col. ill. -- (Food)

Includes index.
Bibliography: p. 31.
04268288 ISBN:1852109254

1. Herbs. 2. Spices. I. Yates, John. II. Title

9358 91JAN23 28/ 1-00539988

HERBS AND SPICES

Linda Illsley

Illustrations by John Yates

Wayland

Food

Apples
Beans and pulses
Bread
Butter
Cakes and biscuits
Cheese
Chocolate
Citrus fruit
Coffee
Eggs
Fish
Herbs and spices
Meat
Milk
Pasta
Potatoes
Rice
Sugar
Tea
Vegetables

All words that appear in **bold** are explained in the glossary on page 30.

Editor: Geraldine Purcell

First published in 1990 by Wayland (Publishers) Limited
61 Western Road, Hove, East Sussex BN3 1JD, England.

© Copyright 1990 Wayland (Publishers) Limited

British Library Cataloguing in Publication Data
Illsley, Linda
Herbs & Spices
1. Culinary herbs 2. Spices
I. Title II. Series
641.357

ISBN 1–85210–925–4

Typeset by Kalligraphic Design Ltd, Horley, Surrey
Printed in Italy by G. Canale & C.S.p.A., Turin
Bound by Casterman S.A., Belgium.

Contents

What are herbs and spices?	4
Herbs and spices in history	6
Pepper	10
Cinnamon and cassia	12
The mints	14
Mustards	16
Vanilla	18
Storing herbs and spices	20
Cooking with herbs and spices	22
Herbs and spices in our diet	24
Herby eggs	26
Vanilla sugar	27
Chicken curry	28
Glossary	30
Books to read	31
Index	32

What are herbs and spices?

Humans have been using plants in their daily lives since the beginning of history. Some have been used as food, others for clothing, for building materials, or for their medicinal or **aromatic** qualities.

Herbs and spices are plants that are used for their taste and aroma (smell). When added to food they add to its flavour, making it taste more interesting. They can turn a dish that tastes dull and boring into a delicious meal. For example, toasted bread with butter is not very appealing,

rosemary

basil

chilli powder

dill seeds

fennel seeds

but add a little cinnamon and you have a delicious combination that is hard to resist. Many drinks are also made with the use of herbs and spices, like mint tea, for example.

There are many different types of herbs all over the world. Some are **cultivated**, and others grow in the wild. The use of herbs varies widely; this book is about the ones used in cooking, which are called culinary, or sweet herbs. Usually the parts of the herb used with food are the leaves and stalks.

Spices come from the seeds, bark, fruit or roots of plants. Some of them can give food a strong flavour and also add a special aroma.

cinnamon sticks

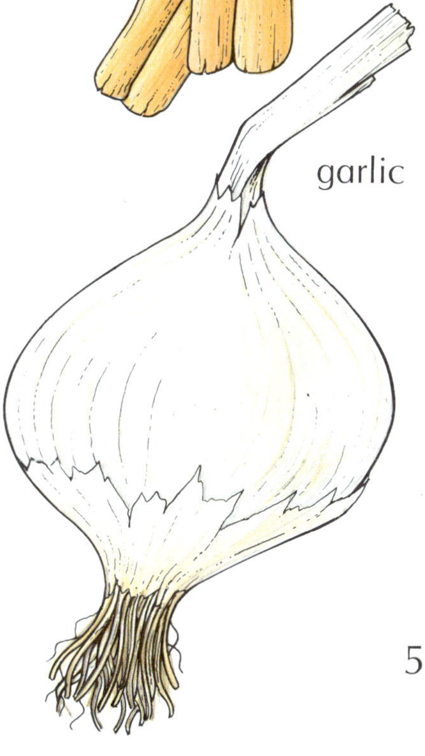
garlic

root ginger

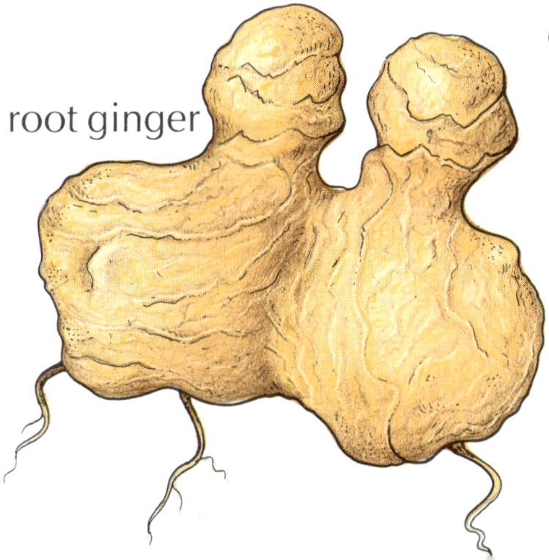

carraway seeds

peppercorns

Herbs and spices in history

The use of herbs and spices is as old as the human race. Scientists have found that long ago, in the **Stone Age**, people were using cumin, poppy seed and angelica. If a plant or shrub smelled or tasted good, people began to use it for a variety of things. The most popular use was in flavouring (seasoning) food. Some ancient peoples believed that certain plants had magical properties and that certain gods preferred the

Many people grow herbs and aromatic plants in their own gardens to use them in cooking.

The spice saffron is very rare and so is quite expensive.

scent of different herbs or spices. It was also believed that witches had their favourite herbs and spices for making magic potions.

Because many people wanted to have herbs and spices they became scarce and very valuable. They were used instead of money for exchange and trade. In other words, when someone wanted to buy a cow, for example, they could pay for it with 2g of saffron or 5g of nutmeg. In the past, people were not able to keep meat fresh for long periods of time, except by drying, salting and spicing it heavily. If the meat started to spoil, the spices would help cover up its bad taste and smell.

Most herbs and spices were first discovered in places where the climate is hot. China, India and Southeast Asia produced many of the most important herbs and spices, like pepper, cinnamon, cassia, cardamom, mace and cloves. Others, like cumin, coriander and fennel, grew

This Indian woman is grinding various spices into powder. Powdered spices are easy to use in cooking because you can add as little or as much as you like.

Left *Spices can be very colourful and have wonderful aromas.*

Below *This girl is sorting out chillies in a market in Thailand.*

in the Mediterranean. Vanilla, allspice, paprika and chillies came from the American continent. Only a few, including horseradish, originated in the colder northern climates.

Many great geographical discoveries happened because of the search for places where spices grew. When **Columbus** landed in America, he thought that he had discovered a new route to India, famous for its valuable spices. This is why the natives of the American continent were called Indians.

Pepper

The pepper plant is a climbing vine, with berries, called peppercorns. Both black and white pepper come from the same plant.

To make black pepper, the berries are picked when they are unripe and still green. Then they are put in the sun to dry. During drying, the berries shrivel and turn brown or black. When these are **ground** you can see black bits from the outside and white bits from the inside.

Above These peppercorns have been dried out and are ready to be ground.

Opposite These peppercorns, growing in Hawaii, are unripe and will be used to make black pepper.

White pepper is made from the ripe berries. The berries are picked, put into sacks and placed in slow-flowing water to soak. After about eight days they become soft. The inside is grey at this stage. The berries are washed once more and put out in the sun to dry. They are left until they turn a creamy-white colour.

Pepper can be added to most dishes. Black pepper is slightly stronger tasting than white. White pepper is useful when cooking light-coloured foods, because the pale specks blend into the food.

Cinnamon and cassia

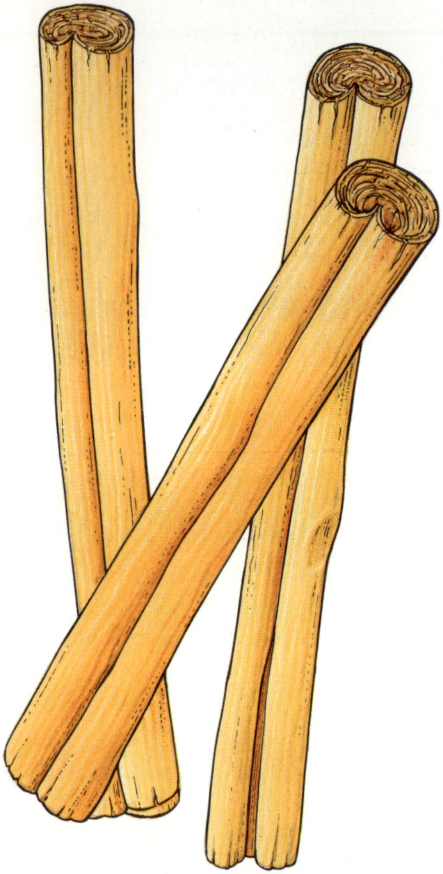

Cinnamon and cassia are two of the oldest known spices. Both have a similar flavour, but cinnamon is considered to be the better of the two. Cassia and cinnamon are used all over the world in the making of sweets. Sometimes they are also added to savoury dishes.

Only a small amount of cinnamon is needed to give flavour to sweet or savoury dishes.

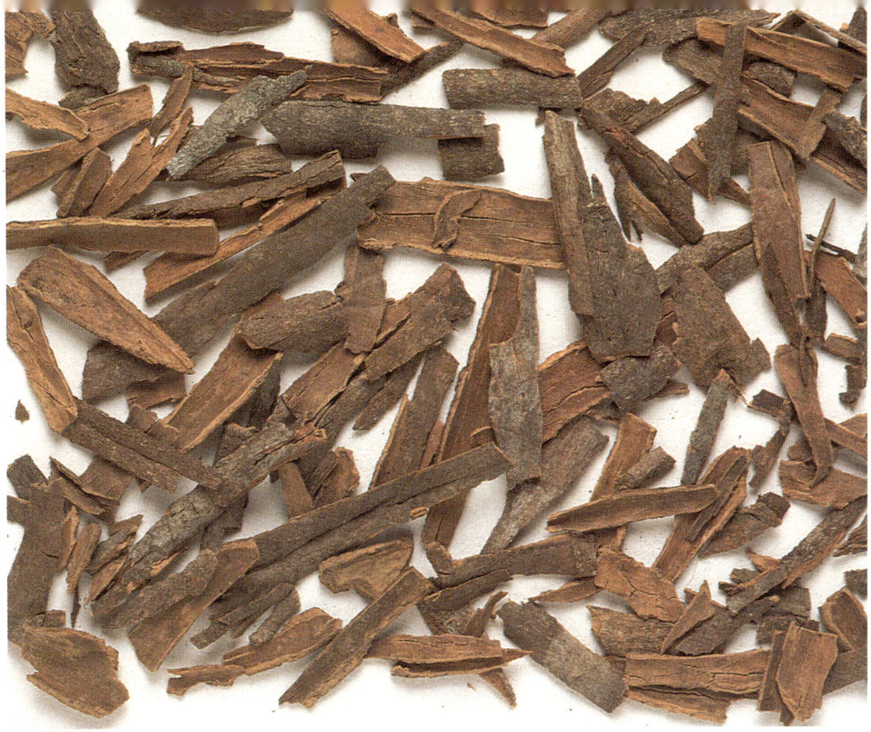

When you buy cassia from a shop it may still look like the bark of the tree – it has to be ground before adding it to food.

They are obtained from the dried bark of the cinnamon or cassia trees. When the trees reach a certain age, the bark is peeled off with special, curved knives and the light-coloured inner bark is cleaned from the corky outer bark. The inner bark curls as it dries, forming a tube, or quill. During drying, the smaller quills are inserted into the larger ones, to form sticks. You can buy them like this or ground into a fine powder.

The mints

Mint, peppermint and spearmint are all very popular herbs. Peppermint oil is used to flavour chewing gum, sweets, toothpaste, and various

Above *A spearmint leaf gives off a very strong minty smell.*

Right *A wild mint plant.*

Left *Iced mint tea is a very refreshing drink.*

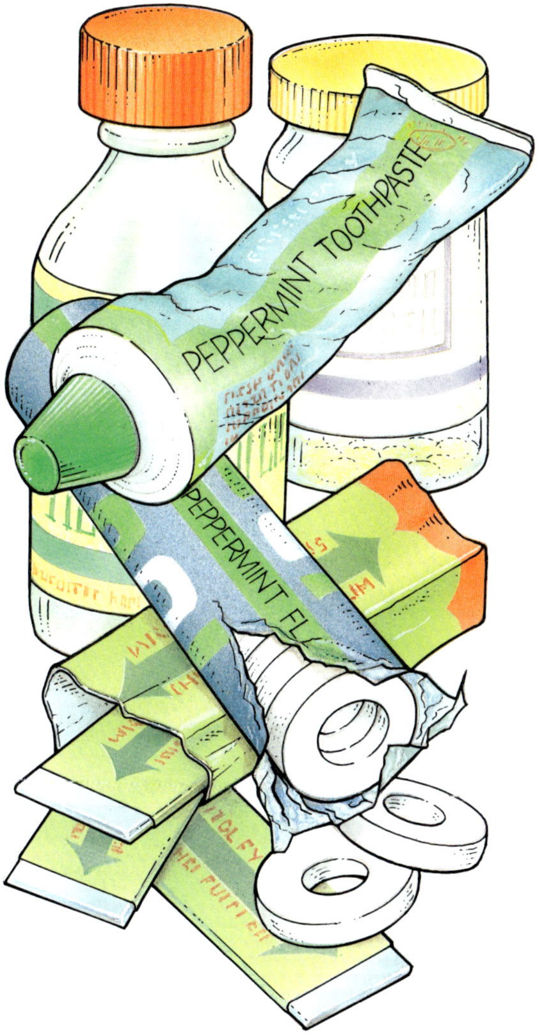

medicines. The smell of the oil is so sharp that it can be used to locate leaks in gas pipes.

Mint tea is a very popular drink in Arab countries. In Britain, mint is made into jellies and sauces to be served with roast lamb. It is also used in salads and vinegars.

Mustards

There are many varieties of mustard seeds. The most common ones are white, yellow, black and brown. Mustard is one of the most commonly used spices in the USA.

You can find mustard in the shops in several different forms. When the seeds are ground into a fine flour it is called powdered dry mustard or hot mustard. It must be moistened with water before use and, once mixed, it should be used within an

Above *Sauerkraut is often eaten with meat, such as pork.*

Right *This woman is picking mustard seeds in India.*

hour, or otherwise its hot flavour is lost.

Prepared mustard, or mustard paste, is a mixture of ground mustard seeds, salt, vinegar and spices. This is the type of mustard used in hot dogs and sandwiches. In France, mustard paste is made by lightly grinding the seeds in vinegar. You can often see little pieces of the seeds in it.

Dry mustard seeds are used to **pickle** food or for seasoning vegetables like **sauerkraut**.

Vanilla

This popular flavouring is obtained from the fruits, or 'beans' of the vanilla vine. These beans have no flavour when picked, for the fragrant aroma develops during the **curing** and **fermenting** process, which can take up to six months. It involves soaking the beans in water

Right The vanilla vine climbs against trees so that it can reach sunlight which helps it grow.

and drying them in the sun until they are **pliable** and deep brown in colour.

There are many **artificial** vanilla products on the market, but the true flavour of the vanilla bean is hard to copy. If you have to use something else instead of vanilla beans, then make sure that the label reads 'vanilla **extract**'. This is obtained by boiling the beans and collecting the steam as a liquid. If it says 'imitation vanilla' then it is made from artificial products and will probably have a bitter and unpleasant after-taste.

Opposite *This is a beautiful example of a vanilla orchid, growing in Costa Rica. When the vanilla orchid dies off, the vanilla beans at its base begin to grow.*

Storing herbs and spices

The way in which herbs and spices are stored at home is very important. If they are stored in open containers they will lose their flavour and aroma. Heat also damages their quality. To keep them at their best, herbs and spices should be stored in airtight glass containers and kept somewhere dry and cool. Dried herbs should be kept away from direct light, so tinted-glass containers are ideal.

The best way to tell if a herb or spice is still

There is a large variety of herbs and spices you can buy. You may have seen a selection at a local food shop or perhaps you have a spice-rack in your kitchen at home.

You can add herbs and spices to savoury preserves, such as ***chutney****.*

fresh is by smelling it. If there is no aroma then it is time to buy new supplies. If the herb is in the form of whole dried leaves such as bay or oregano, then crumble a leaf between your fingers before sniffing it.

Fresh herbs should be kept in the refrigerator, preferably wrapped in a moist cloth, which should be rinsed out every other day. If the herb still has its stems whole, such as parsley or coriander, then it is best to stand the stems in a container with some water. The water should be changed every day to keep the herbs fresh.

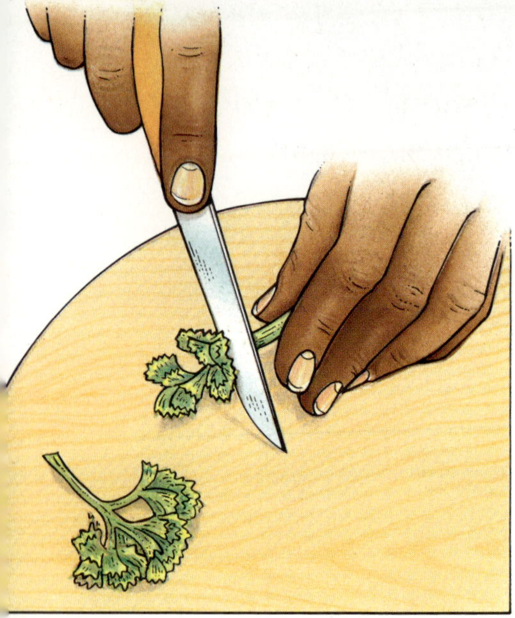

Most herbs, such as parsley, give a better flavour in cooking if they are fresh rather than dried.

Cooking with herbs and spices

When cooking with herbs and spices, the amount added to a dish depends on the taste of the cook. It is a good idea to add just a small amount at a time and to use no more than three spices in any one dish. Herbs and spices should improve the taste of food but not cover it. The exception to this rule is when the dish is meant to be spicy, as with **curry**.

Whenever possible, try to use fresh herbs and spices, and cut or grind them just before you are going to add them to the food. If it is not possible to use them fresh, then remember that dried herbs are much stronger in flavour. If you are following a recipe and need to substitute fresh for dried or vice versa, adjust the amount as follows: 1 tablespoon of dried herbs equals 3 tablespoons of fresh herbs.

Highly-spiced food is very popular in many countries, especially in Asia. These men in Peshawar, Pakistan, are enjoying a spicy meal.

Nowadays, herbs and spices can be purchased in many ways: fresh, dried, **dehydrated**, made into **concentrates**, mixed with salt or sugar, or blended with other spices. However, nothing can really substitute for the fresh products or the fun of making your own combinations and discovering what your favourites are.

Herbs and spices in our diet

The delicious spicy food from this street café in Bangkok, Thailand, probably gives off a very appetizing smell.

Because of the relatively small amount of herbs and spices in our daily diet, their nutritional value is not very important, but they do contain a number of vitamins and minerals.

Some people can only eat very small amounts of salt and sugar. For them herbs and spices are

Meat and vegetables are heavily flavoured by herbs and spices in Indonesian cookery.

especially important, as they make food taste interesting without the use of too much salt and sugar. In fact, we can all benefit by reducing the amount of salt and sugar in our diet. Using herbs and spices instead will complement the wonderful flavours of most foods. And remember, variety is the spice of life!

BRACEBRIDGE PUBLIC LIBRARY

Make sure there is an adult near when you are cooking.

Herby eggs

You will need:

small amounts of these herbs —
chives
tarragon
chervil
1 tablespoon of butter
2 eggs
a pinch of salt
a pinch of pepper

1. Rinse the herbs in cold water and pat them dry with a paper towel. Take the tarragon and chervil leaves off their stalks and chop them coarsely. Chop the chives.

2. Beat the eggs in a bowl and lightly season them with salt and pepper.

3. Heat the butter in a pan. When it has melted, add the eggs and stir them gently with a wooden spoon. When they are almost cooked, add the herbs and stir them in quickly. Serve while hot.

Vanilla sugar

You will need:

250g of granulated sugar
1 glass jar with tight-fitting lid
2 vanilla beans

1. Pour the sugar into the glass jar. Bury the vanilla beans in the sugar.

2. Close the jar tightly and leave the sugar to stand for one week to absorb the flavour of the vanilla. You can add the vanilla sugar to desserts, but remember not to use too much.

Chicken curry

You will need:

6 tablespoons of oil
2 onions, finely chopped
1 clove of garlic, finely chopped
1 tablespoon of fresh root ginger
1 teaspoon of ground turmeric
½ teaspoon of chilli powder
1 teaspoon of ground cumin
1 teaspoon of ground cinnamon
½ teaspoon of ground cardamom
1 teaspoon of ground white pepper
¼ teaspoon of salt
1 medium chicken
280g of natural yoghurt
3 tablespoons of fresh coriander leaves

1. Ask an adult to help you chop the onions, garlic, ginger and coriander, and to cut the chicken into 8 pieces.

2. Heat the oil in a deep casserole dish. Add the onion, garlic and ginger and the powdered spices. Stir gently over a medium heat for 5 minutes.

3. Add the chicken pieces and $\frac{3}{4}$ of the yoghurt. Let the curry simmer for 30 minutes, or until the chicken is cooked thoroughly.

4. Before serving, pour on the rest of the yoghurt and add the coriander. Curry is often served with boiled rice.

Glossary

Aromatic Having a fragrant smell.

Artificial Something that is not natural, usually man-made.

Chutney A highly spiced thick preserve made from vegetables or tropical fruit.

Columbus Christopher Columbus was the Italian explorer who was in the service of Spain, when he landed in the American continent in 1492.

Concentrates Stronger or purer substances obtained by removing water from something.

Cultivated When plants are sown and tended by farmers as their crop.

Curing The processes that keep food fresh by either salting, smoking or pickling it.

Curry A highly spiced dish made with meat, fish or vegetables.

Dehydrated Something that is dehydrated has had the water removed from it.

Extract A substance produced by concentrating the flavour of a plant or animal.

Fermenting To change a substance through heat, moisture or an added ingredient.

Ground Made into a powder.
Pickle To prevent a food from going bad, by putting it in vinegar or salt water.
Pliable When something is soft enough to be easily folded.
Sauerkraut A German dish made from chopped, pickled cabbage.
Stone Age The earliest period of human history when tools and weapons were made of stone.

Books to read

Beans and Pulses by Susanna Miller (Wayland, 1989)
Food and Drink series (Wayland, 1987-9)
Health and Food by Dorothy Baldwin (Wayland, 1988)
Vegetables by Susan Wake (Wayland, 1989)

Index

America (USA) 9, 10, 16
Asia 8

Bangkok (Thailand) 24
Britain 15

China 8
Chutney 21
Columbus, Christopher 9
Cooking 22–3
Costa Rica 18
Curry 22, 28–29

France 16

Hawaii (USA) 10
Herbs
  angelica 6
  bayleaf 21
  fennel 8
  mint 5, 14–15
  oregano 21
  parsley 21
  peppermint 5
  poppyseed 6
  spearmint 14

India 8, 9, 16
Indonesian cookery 25

Peshawar (Pakistan) 23
Pickle 17

Sauerkraut 16, 17
Spices
  allspice 9
  cardamom 8
  cassia 8, 12–13
  chilli 9
  cinnamon, 5, 8, 12–13
  cloves 8
  coriander 8, 21
  cumin 6, 8
  mace 8
  mustard 16–17
  nutmeg 7
  paprika 9
  pepper 8, 10–11
  peppercorn, 10–11
  saffron 7
  vanilla 9, 18–19
Storing 20–21

Thailand 9, 24

Picture acknowledgements

The photographs in this book were provided by: Greg Evans 11, 21; Eye Ubiquitous 12, 13, 23, 24; Hutchison 8; Christine Osborne 7, 9 (both), 15, 16 (right); OSF 6, 10, 14 (left), 18; Peter Stiles COVER; Topham 14, 19, 25; WPL/A. Hasson 16 (left).